The Hound
of the
Baskervilles

BY

Sir Arthur Conan Doyle

EDITED BY
Philip Page & Marilyn Pettit

ILLUSTRATED BY
Philip Page

Published in association with

Hodder & Stoughton

A MEMBER OF THE HODDER HEADLINE GROUP

ABERDEENSHIRE
LIBRARY &
INFORMATION SERVICES
WITHDRAWN
FROM LIBRARY

ALIS
1704099

D0495956

ABERDEENSHIRE LIBRARY AND INFORMATION SERVICE	
1704099	
CAW	366427
LF	£5.99
AD	ALP

Orders: please contact Bookpoint Ltd, 130 Milton Park, Abingdon, Oxon OX14 4SB.
Telephone: (44) 01235 827720, Fax: (44) 01235 400454. Lines are open from 9.00–6.00,
Monday to Saturday, with a 24 hour message answering service. You can also order
through our website at www.hodderheadline.co.uk

British Library Cataloguing in Publication Data
A catalogue record for this title is available from The British Library

ISBN 0 340 78259 5

First published 2001
Impression number   10 9 8 7 6 5 4
Year   2007   2006   2005   2004

Text Copyright © 2001 Philip Page and Marilyn Pettit
Illustrations Copyright © 2001 by Philip Page

All rights reserved. No part of this publication may be reproduced or transmitted in any
form or by any means, electronic or mechanical, including photocopy, recording, or any
information storage and retrieval system, without permission in writing from the publisher
or under licence from the Copyright Licensing Agency Limited. Further details of such
licences (for reprographic reproduction) may be obtained from the Copyright Licensing
Agency Limited, of 90 Tottenham Court Road, London W1T 4LP.

Papers used in this book are natural, renewable and recyclable products. They are made
from wood grown in sustainable forests. The logging and manufacturing processes conform
to the environmental regulations of the country of origin.

Cover illustration by Dave Smith
Typeset by Fakenham Photosetting Ltd, Fakenham, Norfolk
Printed in Great Britain for Hodder & Stoughton Educational, a division of Hodder
Headline, 338 Euston Road, London NW1 3BH by J. W. Arrowsmith Ltd, Bristol

Contents

About the story

Sir Arthur Conan Doyle wrote many Sherlock Holmes stories. The **genre** or type of writing, is detective fiction. It can be called a 'whodunnit'.

Holmes is a detective who solves crimes. None of the other characters can work out the solutions as fast as he can. He is more intelligent than the others and he has to explain to them how he manages to solve the mysteries.

His friend Doctor Watson tries his best to help. He gives Holmes ideas, but he isn't as clever as him.

In this story, there are murders, attempted murders, lies, beatings, and on top of all that, there is the supernatural, in the form of a ghostly hound!

As you read this story, be alert and think fast, because there are lots of clues that will help you find the answer to the evil happenings.

Write your thoughts down as you go along, so that you can decide for yourself, before Sherlock Holmes tells you 'whodunnit'.

Characters in the story

Sherlock Holmes
The famous detective
who solves the crime.

Doctor Watson
Holmes's friend who
helps him solve
the crime.

Doctor Mortimer
A caring man, who
wants to make sure
no one gets hurt.

Sir Charles
Owned Baskerville Hall
and died in strange
circumstances.

Sir Henry
Inherits Baskerville Hall
and is almost killed
by the hound.

Stapleton
Lives with his sister
on the moor near
Baskerville Hall.

Miss Stapleton
Stapleton's beautiful
sister. Sir Henry fell
in love with her.

Barrymore/Mrs Barrymore
Servants at Baskerville Hall.

Lestrade
A policeman.

Selden
An escaped convict.

Laura Lyons
Betrayed and rejected,
she wrote a letter to
Sir Charles which led
to his death!

Frankland
Mrs Lyons' father. His
telescope helped
Watson to solve one
mystery!

Cartwright
A boy who helps
Holmes.

Mr Sherlock Holmes was seated at the breakfast table. I stood upon the hearthrug and picked up the stick which our visitor had left behind the night before. It was a fine, thick piece of wood. Just under the head was a broad silver band. 'To James Mortimer, MRCS, from his friends of the CCH,' was engraved upon it, with the date '1884'.

Well, Watson, what do you make of it?

How did you know what I was doing?

I have a well-polished silver-plated coffee-pot in front of me.

I think Dr Mortimer is a successful elderly medical man, since those who know him gave him this mark of their appreciation.

Excellent!

I think also that **the probability is in favour of his being** a country practitioner who does a great deal of visiting on foot, because this stick has been knocked about. The friends of the CCH I should guess to be the Something Hunt.

MRCS – Member of the Royal College of Surgeons   **the probability ... being** – he is probably

1

A presentation to a doctor is more likely to come from a hospital than from a hunt, and when the initials 'CC' are placed before that hospital, the words 'Charing Cross' suggest themselves. And he left five years ago.

Dear Watson, there emerges a young fellow under thirty, **amiable**, **unambitious**, absent-minded, and the possessor of a favourite dog. The marks of his teeth **are very plainly visible**. The dog's jaw is too broad for a terrier and not broad enough for a mastiff.

It is a curly-haired spaniel.

How can you possibly be so sure of that?

I see the dog on our very doorstep, and there is the ring of its owner.

He was a very tall, thin man, with a long nose like a beak, which shot out between two keen, grey eyes, set closely together and sparkling brightly from behind a pair of gold-rimmed glasses. His frock-coat was dingy and his trousers frayed. Though young, his long back was already bowed. As he entered his eyes fell upon the stick.

amiable – friendly   **unambitious** – doesn't want to get on in life   **are ... visible** – can be seen

confronted with – faced with

Dr Mortimer begins to explain the problem, by telling a frightening story from long ago.

I have in my pocket a manuscript. This family paper was **committed to my care** by Sir Charles Baskerville whose sudden and tragic death some three months ago created so much excitement in Devonshire. It is the statement of a certain legend which runs in the Baskerville family. I will read it to you.

This Manor of Baskerville was held by Hugo of that name. Hugo came to love the daughter of a yeoman, who held lands near the Baskerville estate. But the young maiden would ever avoid him, for she feared his evil name.

Hugo, with five or six of his idle and wicked companions, stole down upon the farm and carried off the maiden. When they had brought her to the Hall, the maiden was placed in an upper chamber. In her fear, by the aid of the growth of ivy, she came down from under the **eaves** and so homeward across the moor.

Some time later Hugo left his guests to carry food and drink to his **captive**, and so found the cage empty. He became as one that hath a devil. He cried aloud that he would that very night **render** his body and soul to the Powers of Evil if he might but overtake the wench.

One more wicked or more drunken than the rest cried out that they should put the hounds upon her. Hugo **swung them to the line** and so off full cry over the moor. The **revellers**, thirteen in number, took horse and started pursuit.

---

committed to my care – given to me to look after   **eaves** – roof   **captive** – prisoner
render – give up
swung them to the line – set the dogs off after the girl   **revellers** – drunkards

They passed one of the night shepherds and cried to him to know if he had seen the hunt.

He said, 'Hugo Baskerville passed me upon his black mare, and there ran **mute** behind him such a hound of hell as God forbid should ever be at my heels.'

Three rode forward. The moon was shining bright. There lay the unhappy maid, dead of fear and **fatigue**.

Standing over Hugo there stood a foul thing, a great, black beast, shaped like a hound, yet larger than any hound that ever mortal eye has rested on. The thing tore the throat out of Hugo Baskerville. It turned its blazing eyes and dripping jaws upon them. One died that very night, the other **twain** were broken men.

Such is the tale of the coming of the hound which is said to have plagued the family ever since.

---

mute – silent   **fatigue** – extreme tiredness   **twain** – two

Dr Mortimer goes on to give some facts and opinions about the death of Sir Charles Baskerville.

Do you not find it interesting?

To a collector of fairy-tales.

This is the *Devon County Chronicle* of June 14th of this year.

'Sir Charles Baskerville was in the habit every night before going to bed of walking down the famous Yew Alley of Baskerville Hall. On the 4th of June Sir Charles **had declared his intention of starting** next day for London. That night he went out as usual for his walk. He never returned. At twelve o'clock Barrymore went in search of his master. Half-way down this walk there is a gate which leads out on to the moor. There were indications that Sir Charles had stood for some little time here. He then proceeded down the Alley, and it was at the far end of it that his body was discovered. One fact which has not been explained is the statement of Barrymore that his master's footprints altered from the time that he passed the moor-gate, and that he appeared from **thence** onwards to have been walking upon his toes.'

This article contains all the public facts? Then let me have the private ones.

had declared his intention of starting – said he would set off
thence – then

I saw a good deal of Sir Charles Baskerville. He had taken this legend to heart. Nothing would **induce** him to go out upon the moor at night. He was convinced that a dreadful fate overhung his family. On more than one occasion he asked me whether I had ever seen any strange creature or heard the **baying** of a hound. He **confided to my keeping** that narrative which I read to you.

It was at my advice that Sir Charles was about to go to London. I thought that a few months among the distractions of the town would send him back a new man. Mr Stapleton, a mutual friend, was of the same opinion.

On the night of Sir Charles's death I checked and **corroborated** all the facts. Sir Charles lay on his face, his arms out, his fingers dug into the ground, and his features convulsed. There was no physical injury of any kind.

One false statement was made by Barrymore at the inquest.

He said that there were no traces upon the ground round the body. He did not observe any.

But I did. They were the footprints of a gigantic hound!

induce – persuade   **baying** – howling   **confided to my keeping** – gave me
corroborated – agreed

luminous and spectral – shining and ghostly   heir – the person who gets the money and house

Later that day Holmes shares his ideas with Watson about Sir Charles's death.

Why should a man walk on tiptoe down the alley? He was running, Watson – desperately until he burst his heart and fell dead. Only a man who had lost his wits would have run from the house instead of towards it.

Whom was he waiting for? The man was elderly, the ground was damp and the night **inclement**. Is it natural that he should stand for five or ten minutes? I think it unlikely that he waited at the moor-gate every evening. He avoided the moor. That night he waited there. It was the night before he was to take his departure for London.

inclement – was cold and wet

The next day Sir Henry Baskerville arrives. He has a few puzzles to tell Holmes.

I understand you think out little puzzles. I've had one this morning. It was this letter.

As you value your life or your reason keep away from the moor.

Have you yesterday's Times, Watson?

Don't you see now whence these words have been taken?

Someone cut out this message with scissors. I want to know why the word 'moor' should have been written.

Because he could not find it in print!

Has anything else of interest happened to you since you have been in London?

reason – mind   *Times* – a newspaper

10

I hope that to lose one of your boots is not part of the ordinary routine of life over here. I **put them outside my door** last night and there was only one in the morning. I only bought the pair last night. I have never had them on.

It is time that you gave me a full account of what we are driving at.

Our scientific friend presented the whole case.

We now have to decide whether it is or is not advisable for you to go to Baskerville Hall.

There is no devil in hell and there is no man upon earth who can prevent me from going to the home of my people.

I am going back right away to my hotel. Come round and lunch with us at two.

put them outside my door – to be polished

Holmes is sure that somebody has been watching Sir Henry since he arrived in London. He and Watson follow Sir Henry and the doctor as soon as they leave.

Dr Mortimer and Baskerville were still visible. Keeping a hundred yards behind, we followed into Oxford Street and so down Regent Street. Holmes gave a little cry of satisfaction.

There's our man!

I was aware of a bushy black beard and a pair of piercing eyes through the side window of the cab. The trapdoor at the top flew up, something was screamed to the driver, and the cab flew madly off.

Holmes dashed in pursuit but the start was too great and already the cab was out of sight.

We are dealing with a clever man, Watson.

Could you swear to that man's face within the cab?

I could swear only to the beard.

And so could I – from which I gather it was a false one.

Holmes and Watson meet Sir Henry at his hotel and make plans to travel to Baskerville Hall.

As we came round the top of the stairs we had run up against Sir Henry himself. His face was flushed with anger, and he held up an old, dusty boot in one of his hands.

I only had three pairs in the world—the new brown, the old black and the patent leathers, which I am wearing. Last night they took one of my brown ones, and today they have sneaked one of the black.

What do you make of it?

Well, I don't **profess** to understand it yet.

We had a pleasant luncheon. It was in the private sitting room to which we afterwards **repaired** that Holmes asked Baskerville what were his intentions.

To go to Baskerville Hall.

I think your decision is a wise one. You did not know that you were followed this morning from my house?

By whom?

That, unfortunately is what I cannot tell you.

profess – claim   **repaired** – went to sit down

Sir Henry, you must take with you someone, a trusty man, who will be always by your side. If my friend would undertake it there is no man who is better worth having at your side when you are in a tight place.

I will come with pleasure.

And you will report very carefully to me.

We had risen to depart when Baskerville gave a cry of triumph, and diving into one of the corners of the room he drew a brown boot from under a cabinet.

Then on Saturday we shall meet at the 10.30 train from Paddington.

My missing boot!

We had a line of **inexplicable incidents** all within the limits of two days, which included the receipt of the printed letter, the black-bearded spy in the **hansom**, the loss of the new brown boot, the loss of the old black boot, and now the return of the new brown boot.

Holmes sat in silence as we drove back to Baker Street. I knew that his mind was busy.

inexplicable incidents – things that can't be explained
hansom – carriage

Watson, Sir Henry and Dr Mortimer arrive at the dark and gloomy Baskerville Hall, where there are further mysteries waiting for them.

Sir Henry Baskerville and Dr Mortimer were ready upon the **appointed** day. The journey was a swift and pleasant one. The train pulled up at a small station, and we all descended. Outside, a wagonette with a pair of **cobs** was waiting.

What's this?

There's a convict escaped from Princetown, sir. He's been out three days now, and the watchers watch every road and station.

Who is he then?

Selden, the Notting Hill murderer.

In front of us rose the **huge expanse** of the moor. It set us shivering.

appointed – agreed   **cobs** – horses   **huge expanse** – big stretch

Baskerville Hall!

Welcome to Baskerville Hall.

Would you wish dinner to be served at once, sir?

Is it ready?

In a very few minutes, sir.

The dining-room was a place of shadow and gloom. We talked a little and I was glad when the meal was over.

If it suits you, we will **retire** early tonight, and perhaps things may seem more cheerful in the morning.

I drew aside my curtains before I went to bed. I saw beyond the trees the long, low curve of the **melancholy** moor. I found myself **weary and yet wakeful**.

Then suddenly, there came a sound, the sob of a woman. I sat up in bed and listened, but there came no other sound save the chiming clock and the rustle of ivy on the wall.

retire – go to bed   **melancholy** – sad   **weary ... wakeful** – tired but couldn't sleep

Next morning Watson sets off on a walk and meets Stapleton, who lives close by. He has some ideas about the death of Sir Charles. And the horrible cry of the hound is heard!

Sir Henry had papers to examine after breakfast, so that the time was **propitious for my excursion**. It was a pleasant walk along the edge of the moor. Suddenly my thoughts were interrupted.

Dr Watson.

I am Stapleton, of Merripit House.

Sir Henry is none the worse for his journey? We were all rather afraid that after the sad death of Sir Charles the new baronet might refuse to live here.

You know the legend of the fiend dog? The story took a great hold on the imagination of Sir Charles, and I have no doubt that it led to his tragic end. I knew that his heart was weak.

You think that some dog pursued Sir Charles, and that he died of fright?

Have you any better explanation?

I have not come to any conclusion.

Has Mr Sherlock Holmes?

The words took away my breath for an instant.

propitious for my excursion – suitable for my walk

17

If you are here, then it follows that Mr Holmes is interesting himself in the matter.

I am simply here upon a visit to my friend Sir Henry.

Excellent!

Perhaps you will spare an hour that I may have the pleasure of introducing my sister.

I have only been here two years. We came shortly after Sir Charles settled.

That is the Grimpen Mire. A false step means death to man or beast. Only yesterday I saw one of the moor ponies wander into it. He never came out. There are one or two paths which a very active man can take. I have found them out.

What is that?

A long, low moan swept across the moor. It filled the whole air. From a dull murmur it swelled into a deep roar and then sank back into a melancholy throbbing murmur once again.

The peasants say it is the Hound of the Baskervilles calling for its prey.

I looked around with a chill of fear in my heart.

Dr Watson meets Miss Stapleton—the sister. She has some very puzzling words of warning, and then behaves in a strange way!

A small fly or moth had fluttered across our path. Stapleton was rushing in pursuit. I heard the sound of steps and turning round found a woman near me. I could not doubt that this was Miss Stapleton.

Go straight back to London.

Why should I go back?

I cannot explain. Never set foot upon the moor again. Hush, my brother is coming! Not a word of what I have said.

Hullo, Beryl. You have introduced yourselves I see.

Yes, I was telling Sir Henry . . .

My name is Dr Watson.

We have been talking at cross purposes. You will come on and see Merripit House?

A short walk brought us to it, a **bleak** moorland house. As I looked from their windows, I could not but **marvel** at what could have brought this highly educated man and this beautiful woman to live in such a place.

I **resisted all pressure** to stay for lunch and I set off at once upon my return journey.

Before I had reached the road I was astounded to see Miss Stapleton.

I have run all the way to cut you off, Dr Watson. Please forget the words I said.

Tell me why it was that you were so eager that Sir Henry should return to London?

A woman's **whim**. You make too much of it, Dr Watson.

Why should you not wish your brother to overhear what you said?

My brother is very anxious to have the Hall **inhabited**. I have done my duty now and I will say no more! Goodbye!

She turned and had disappeared in a few minutes among the scattered boulders, while I, full of fears, pursued my way to Baskerville Hall.

bleak – chilly and gloomy   **marvel** – wonder   **resisted all pressure** – said no to their invitation
whim – sudden idea   **inhabited** – lived in

Dr Watson meets some of the neighbours, and is disturbed by Barrymore creeping around in the middle of the night.

From this point on I will follow the course of events by **transcribing** my own letters to Mr Sherlock Holmes. One page is missing, but otherwise they are exactly as written.

Baskerville Hall

My Dear Holmes,
Stapleton came over to call upon Baskerville on that first day, and the very next morning he took us both to show us the spot where the legend of the wicked Hugo is supposed to have **had its origin**.

On our way back we stayed to lunch at Merripit House, and it was there that Sir Henry **made the acquaintance of** Miss Stapleton. He appeared to be strongly attracted by her.

One other neighbour I have met is Mr Frankland. He is an elderly man. He has an excellent telescope with which he lies upon the roof of his own house and sweeps the moor all day in the hope of catching a glimpse of the escaped convict.

transcribing – writing down   **had its origin** – started   **made the acquaintance of** – met

And now let me tell you about the Barrymores. Last night, I was **aroused** by a **stealthy** step passing my room. I rose, opened my door and peeped out. A long dark shadow was trailing down the passage with a candle.

It was Barrymore.

He entered one of the rooms. I peeped round the corner of the door.

For some minutes he stood watching. Then he gave a deep groan and put out the light.

I have had a long talk with Sir Henry this morning and we have made a plan.

aroused – woken up   **stealthy** – quiet

22

Stapleton gets very angry with Sir Henry, because he is talking to his sister! He shouts and behaves badly. Later on, he apologises! Neither Sir Henry, nor Watson understand what is going on!

Baskerville Hall

My Dear Holmes,

Today Sir Henry put on his hat and prepared to go out. I did the same …
It put me in a most awkward position, and before I had made up my mind he was gone. I imagined what my feelings would be if I had to return to you, and to confess that some **misfortune had occurred through my disregard for your instructions**.
I set off in the direction of Merripit House. I mounted a hill.

My dear fellow, I must go out alone.

Then I saw him at once. A lady was at his side who could only be Miss Stapleton. Sir Henry suddenly drew Miss Stapleton to his side. His arm was around her. Next moment I saw them spring apart. Stapleton was the cause. It seemed to me that Stapleton was abusing Sir Henry. Finally Stapleton turned upon his heel and beckoned to his sister, who walked off by the side of her brother.
What all this meant I could not imagine. I ran down the hill and met the baronet at the bottom.

misfortune had occurred – accident had happened
through my disregard for your instructions – because I didn't listen to you

What has he against me? He would not so much as let me touch the tips of her fingers.

I offered to marry her, but before she could answer down came this brother of hers running at us with a face on him like a madman.

I was completely puzzled myself.

Our **conjectures were set at rest** by a visit from Stapleton himself that very afternoon. He had come to offer apologies for his rudeness of the morning, and the **breach is quite healed**. We are to dine at Merripit House next Friday as a sign of it.

And now I pass on to the mystery of the sobs.

It was by two nights' work for on the first we **drew entirely blank**.

One struck and two. We heard the creak of a step in the passage. The baronet gently opened his door.

We stole along.

He passed through the same door as before. We found him crouching at the window, candle in hand.

conjectures were set at rest – guesses were stopped
breach ... healed – quarrel has been sorted out   **drew entirely blank** – found nothing out

24

Sir Henry and Dr Watson set out to try to catch Selden. They have a very frightening experience on the moor and Watson sees a strange man watching them.

By thunder, I am going out to take that man! Get your revolver.

Are you armed?

I have a hunting-crop.

There rose suddenly out of the vast gloom of the moor that strange cry—a long, deep mutter then a rising howl and then the sad moan. Again and again it sounded. It died away and an absolute silence closed in on us.

Good Heaven's, what's that, Watson?

They say it is the cry of the Hound of the Baskervilles.

It rose and fell with the wind. Isn't that the direction of the great Grimpen Mire?

I don't think that I am a coward, Watson, but that sound seemed to freeze my very blood.

Shall we turn back?

No.

We stumbled slowly along in the darkness with the black loom of the **craggy** hills around us, and the yellow speck of light burning steadily in front.

craggy – rocky

Barrymore asks Watson and Sir Henry not to tell the police about Selden. He also has an exciting piece of information about Sir Charles's death.

Now, I am to trust once more to my **recollections**, aided by the diary which I kept at the time.

October 16th
This morning after breakfast, Barrymore asked to speak with Sir Henry in his study. After a time the baronet opened the door . . .

Barrymore considers that he has a **grievance**. He thinks it was unfair on our part to hunt his brother-in-law down when he, of his own free will, had told us the secret.

In a very few days, he will be on his way to South America. I beg of you not to let the police know that he is still on the moor. You can't tell on him without getting my wife and me into trouble.

I don't feel as if I could give the man up. All right, Barrymore, you can go.

You've been so kind to us, sir. I know something about poor Sir Charles's death. I know why he was at the gate at that hour. It was to meet a woman. I can't give you the name, but I can give you the initials. 'L.L.'

Your uncle had a letter that morning addressed in a woman's **hand**. My wife was cleaning out Sir Charles's study. She found a burned letter in the grate. A postscript at the end of the letter said:

Please, please, burn this letter, and be at the gate by ten o'clock.
L.L.

recollections – memory   **grievance** – complaint   **hand** – handwriting

Watson finds out who the mysterious woman with the initials 'L.L.' is. He also hears that there is another man on the moor—possibly the one he saw the night he chased the convict, Selden.

October 17th

All day today the rain poured down. In the evening I put on my waterproof and I walked upon the **sodden** moor. I was overtaken by Dr Mortimer.

Can you tell me the name of any woman whose initials are L.L.?

There is Laura Lyons. She lives in Coombe Tracey. She is Frankland's daughter. She married an artist. Her father refused to have anything to do with her.

Tomorrow morning I shall find my way to Coombe Tracey, and if I can see this Mrs Laura Lyons, a long step will have been made towards clearing one incident in this chain of mysteries.

I have only one other incident to record. My conversation with Barrymore.

Has this relation of yours departed?

I've not heard of him since I left out food for him three days ago.

Did you see him then?

No sir, but the food was gone when next I went that way ... unless it was the other man who took it.

sodden – soaking wet

29

Selden told me of him, sir. He's in hiding, too, but he's not a convict. At first he thought he was the police.

I stared at him.

And where did he say that he lived?

Among the old houses on the hillside.

But how about his food?

Selden found out that he has got a lad who works for him and brings him all he needs.

I walked over to the black window. There, in that hut upon the moor, seems to lie the problem which has **vexed me so sorely**. I swear that another day shall not have passed before I have done all that man can do to reach the heart of the mystery.

vexed me so sorely – bothered me so much

30

Watson visits Mrs Laura Lyons and finds out the truth about the letter and the meeting with Sir Charles, just before he died.

It was about the late Sir Charles Baskerville that I have come here to see you. Did you **correspond with** Sir Charles?

Once or twice.

Have you ever met him?

Once or twice.

There were several gentlemen who knew my sad history and **united** to help me. One was Mr Stapleton. It was through him that Sir Charles learned about my affairs.

Did you ever write to Sir Charles asking him to meet you?

No.

Surely **your memory deceives you**. I could even quote a passage of your letter. It ran 'Please, please, as you are a gentleman, burn this letter and be at the gate ...'

Is there no such thing as a gentleman?

He did burn the letter. Sometimes a letter **may be legible** even when burned.

correspond with – write to   **united** – got together
your memory deceives you – you've forgotten   **may be legible** – can still be read

You wrote it?

Yes, I asked him to meet me.

But why at such an hour?

Because I had only just learned that he was going to London next day and might be away for months.

Why a **rendezvous** in the garden?

Do you think a woman could go alone at that hour to a bachelor's house

What happened when you did get there?

I never went.

You will know that I made a **rash** marriage. There was a **prospect of my regaining my freedom if certain expenses could be met**. I knew Sir Charles's generosity. I thought that if he heard the story from my own lips he would help me.

How is it that you did not go?

Because I received help from another source.

Why did you not write to Sir Charles and explain this?

So I should have done had I not seen his death in the paper next morning.

I could proceed no further, but must turn back to that other clue which was to be **sought** for among the stone huts upon the moor.

rendezvous – meeting   **rash** – foolish   **prospect ... be met** – chance of getting free if I had some money   **sought** – looked

Watson meets Mr Frankland who gives him the best clue yet about the mystery man living in the stone huts on the moor.

Luck had been against us again and again in this inquiry, but now at last it came to my aid.

What about the convict on the moor?

You don't mean that you know where he is?

I know because I have seen the messenger who takes him food.

My heart sank for Barrymore.

His food is taken to him by a child. I see him every day through my telescope.

Here was luck indeed! Barrymore had said that our unknown was supplied by a boy.

It was on his track and not upon the convict's that Frankland had stumbled.

Every day and sometimes twice a day, I have been able—but wait a moment, is that something moving upon that hillside?

Come sir!

The telescope stood upon the **flat leads** of the house. Frankland clapped his eye to it and gave a cry of satisfaction.

There he was for sure, a small **urchin** with a little bundle upon his shoulder. He looked round him. Then he vanished over the hill.

flat leads – roof   **urchin** – scruffy boy

33

I succeeded in dissuading him from his announced intention of walking home with me. I kept to the road as long as his eye was on me, then, made for the stony hill over which the boy had disappeared.

The barren scene, the sense of loneliness, and the mystery and urgency of my task all struck a chill into my heart. The boy was nowhere to be seen.

There was a circle of old stone huts and in the middle of them there was one which **retained sufficient** roof to act as a screen against the weather.

The place was empty. In the middle a flat stone served the purpose of a table and upon this stood a small cloth bundle. It contained a loaf of bread, a tinned tongue, and two tins of peaches. My heart leaped to see a sheet of paper with writing upon it.

Dr Watson has gone to Coombe Tracey.

I succeeded ... with me – I managed to persuade him (Frankland) to let me walk home alone
retained sufficient – had enough

It was I then, and not Sir Henry, who was being dogged by this secret man. Was he our enemy or was he by chance our guardian angel? I swore that I would not leave the hut until I knew.

Far away came the sharp clink of a boot striking upon a stone.

I shrank back into the darkest corner and cocked my pistol in my pocket.

There was a long pause. A shadow fell across the opening of the hut.

It's a lovely evening, my dear Watson.

Holmes!

Watson finds out the truth about Miss Stapleton. He also learns that they are dealing with murder!

I am glad that you are here.

Tell me the result of your visit to Mrs Laura Lyons.

I had to repeat some of it twice before he was satisfied.

You are aware that a close **intimacy** exists between this lady and Stapleton? They meet, they write. If only I could use it to **detach the wife**.

His wife?

The lady who has passed here as Miss Stapleton is his wife.

But why?

Because he foresaw that she would be very much more useful to him in the character of a free woman.

It is he then who is our enemy—it is he who dogged us in London? And the warning must have come from her!

Exactly.

If this woman is his wife, where does Mrs Laura Lyons come in?

intimacy – friendship   **detach the wife** – get his wife away from him

I did not know about a **projected** divorce between herself and her husband. Regarding Stapleton as an unmarried man, she counted no doubt upon becoming his wife. It must be our first duty to see her tomorrow.

One last question, Holmes. What is he after?

It is murder, Watson—cold-blooded, deliberate murder.

A terrible scream—a yell of horror burst out of the silence of the moor.

That frightful cry turned the blood to ice in my veins.

projected – planned

The hound chases a man to his death. Watson and Holmes think, at first, that it is Sir Henry, but they are surprised to find that it is someone else. Stapleton is also surprised—and disappointed!

The hound! If we are too late!

Blindly we ran through the gloom, blundering against boulders, forcing our way through bushes, panting up hills and rushing down slopes, heading always in the direction whence those dreadful sounds had come.

What is that?

A low moan had fallen upon our ears. On that side, a ridge of rocks ended in a sheer cliff which overlooked a stone-strewn slope. On its jagged face was spread-eagled some dark object. It was a man face downwards upon the ground.

The body of Sir Henry! There was no chance of either of us forgetting that tweed suit.

Where is this hound which drove him to his death? And Stapleton? He shall answer for this.

The man has a beard! It is not the baronet—it is my neighbour, the convict!

In an instant it was all clear to me. The baronet had handed his old **wardrobe** to Barrymore. Barrymore had passed it on in order to help Selden in his escape. Boots, shirt, cap—it was all Sir Henry's.

wardrobe – clothes

It is clear that the hound has been laid on from some article of Sir Henry's—the boot in the hotel, in all possibility—and so ran this man down.

A greater mystery to me is why this hound should be loose tonight. Stapleton would not let it go unless he had reason to think that Sir Henry would be there.

A figure was approaching us. I could **distinguish** the **jaunty** walk of the naturalist.

Stapleton turned a ghastly face upon us, but he had overcome his amazement and disappointment.

Who—who's this?

Selden—the man who escaped from Princetown.

My friend and I were strolling on the moor when we heard a cry.

I heard a cry also. I was uneasy about Sir Henry. I had suggested that he should come over. When he did not come I was surprised. I naturally became **alarmed** for his safety when I heard cries upon the moor.

distinguish – make out   **jaunty** – cheerful   **alarmed** – worried

Holmes notices something interesting about a family **portrait** in Baskerville Hall.

Sir Henry was more pleased than surprised to see Sherlock Holmes. Over supper, we explained to the baronet as much of our experience as it seemed he should know.

But how about the case?

I think I shall be in a position to make the situation rather more clear to you before long.

We heard the hound on the moor. I think I will muzzle him and chain him all right if you will give me your help.

He stopped suddenly.

What is it?

These are a really fine series of portraits.

They are all family portraits, I presume.

Every one.

That is the wicked Hugo, who started the Hound of the Baskervilles.

portrait – painting of somebody

When Sir Henry had gone to his room, Holmes led me back into the banqueting-hall, his bedroom candle in his hand.

Do you see anything there?

Good heavens!

The face of Stapleton had sprung out of the canvas.

Ha, you see it now.

It might be his portrait.

The fellow is a Baskerville—that is evident.

With designs upon the succession.

With designs upon the succession – with plans to get Baskerville Hall

Holmes and Watson pretend to return to London. They visit Mrs Laura Lyons and meet the police detective, Lestrade, who has come to help them make an arrest.

You are engaged to dine with our friends the Stapletons tonight.

I hope that you will come also.

Watson and I must go to London.

I hoped that you were going to see me through this business.

Trust me and do exactly what I tell you. Tell your friends that urgent business required us to be in town.

Drive to Merripit House. Send back your **trap**. Let them know that you intend to walk home.

And as you value your life, do not go across the moor in any direction save along the straight path which leads from Merripit House to the Grimpen Road.

A couple of hours later we were at the station of Coombe Tracey. A small boy was waiting upon the platform.

Take this train to town, Cartwright. Send a **wire** to Sir Henry Baskerville in my name. And ask at the station office if there is a message for me.

trap – carriage   **wire** – telegram

Ask me what you like, and there is nothing which I shall hold back.

When I wrote the letter I never dreamed of any harm to the old gentleman.

The sending of this letter was suggested to you by Stapleton?

He dictated it.

He dissuaded you from keeping the appointment?

He told me it would hurt his self-respect that any other man should find the money for such an object, and that though he was a poor man himself he would devote his last penny to removing the obstacles which divided us.

He made you swear to say nothing about your appointment with Sir Charles?

He said that the death was a very mysterious one, and that I should certainly be suspected if the facts came out.

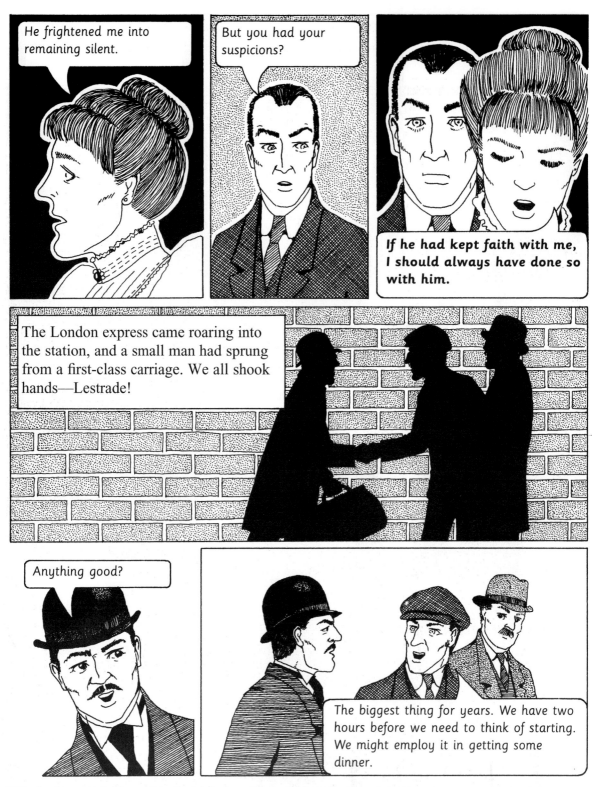

If he had . . . with him – If he hadn't let me down, I would have stuck by him.

The three men, Holmes, Watson and Lestrade, lie in wait for what might happen to Sir Henry. They are nervous, because it is foggy and they can hardly see what is going on.

The great ordeal was in front of us. My nerves thrilled with anticipation. It was a relief to me when we knew we were drawing near to the Hall and to the scene of the action. We did not drive up to the door, but got down near the gate of the drive.

We started to Merripit House.

What's the game now?

A waiting game.

It does not seem a cheerful place.

I see the lights of a house ahead.

Merripit House.

We moved cautiously along the track as if we were bound for the house, but Holmes halted us.

This will do. These rocks upon the right make an admirable screen. We shall make our little ambush here.

Creep forward quietly and see what they are doing—but don't let them know they are being watched.

I tiptoed down the path and stooped behind the low wall which surrounded the orchard. There were only two men in the room, Sir Henry and Stapleton. As I watched them, Stapleton rose and left the room.

I heard the creak of a door and the sound of boots on gravel. I saw the naturalist pause at the door of an outhouse in the corner of the orchard. A key turned in a lock and as he passed in there was a curious scuffling noise. He was only a minute or so inside then I heard the key turn once more and he re-entered the house. I saw him re-join his guest.

I crept back to where my companions were waiting.

Over the great Grimpen Mire there hung a dense, white fog. It was drifting slowly in our direction. The moon shone on it and it looked like a great shimmering ice-field.

It's moving towards us, Watson.

Is that serious?

Very serious indeed. Our success and even his life may depend upon his coming out before the fog is over the path.

Every minute that white woolly plain which covered one half of the moor was drifting closer and closer to the house.

If he isn't out in a quarter of an hour the path will be covered. In half an hour we won't be able to see our hands in front of us.

Shall we move farther back upon higher ground?

Yes, I think it would be as well.

So as the fog-bank flowed onwards we fell back before it until we were half a mile from the house.

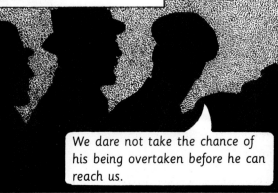

We dare not take the chance of his being overtaken before he can reach us.

Sir Henry is saved from the hound by Holmes, Watson and Lestrade.

A sound of quick steps broke the silence of the moor. There stepped the man whom we were awaiting. He came swiftly along the path, passed close to where we lay and went on up the long slope behind us.

Look out!
It's coming!

I was at Holmes's elbow, and I glanced at his face. It was pale, his eyes shining brightly. But suddenly they started in a rigid, fixed stare. Lestrade gave a yell of terror. I sprang to my feet, my hand grasping my pistol, my mind paralysed by the dreadful shape which had sprung out upon us from the shadows of the fog.

A hound it was, an enormous coal-black hound, but not such a hound as mortal eyes have ever seen.

Fire burst from its open mouth, its eyes glowed with a smouldering glare, its muzzle and hackles were outlined in flickering flame.

With long bounds the huge black creature was leaping down the track, following hard upon the footsteps of our friend. So paralysed were we by the **apparition** that we allowed it to pass before we recovered our nerve.

Then Holmes and I both fired and the creature gave a hideous howl which showed that one at least had hit him.

Far away on the path we saw Sir Henry looking back, his face white in the moonlight, his hands raised in horror, glaring helplessly at the frightful thing which was hunting him down.

As we flew up the track we heard scream after scream from Sir Henry and the deep roar of the hound. I was in time to see the beast spring upon its victim, hurl him to the ground and worry at his throat.

apparition – sight

The next instant Holmes had emptied five barrels of his revolver into the creature's **flank**.

With a last howl of agony and a vicious snap in the air it rolled upon its back, four feet pawing furiously and then fell limp upon its side. The giant hound was dead.

We helped him to a rock where he sat shivering with his face buried in his hands.

flank – side   **phosphorus** – a chemical which glows in the dark

Stapleton escapes. Mrs Stapleton is found beaten and tied.

We retraced our steps down the path. The front door was open so we rushed in and hurried from room to room. There was no light save in the dining-room. No sign could we see of the man whom we were chasing. On the upper floor one of the bedroom doors was locked.

Holmes struck the door just over the lock and it flew open.

In a minute we had torn off the gag, **unswathed** the bonds and Mrs Stapleton sank upon the floor in front of us.

I saw the clear red **weal** of a whip-lash across her neck. She shot her arms out and we saw with horror that they were all mottled with bruises.

unswathed – untied   **weal** – scar

Tell us where we shall find him.

There is an old tin mine on an island in the heart of the Mire. It was there that he kept his hound. That is where he would fly.

We left Lestrade, while Holmes and I went back with the baronet to Baskerville Hall.

The story of the Stapletons could no longer be withheld from him. He took the blow bravely when he learned the truth about the woman he had loved.

The shock of the night's adventures had shattered his nerves, and before morning he lay in a high fever under the care of Dr Mortimer.

Mrs Stapleton shows Holmes and Watson where she thinks her husband might have met his death!

On the morning after the death of the hound the fog had lifted and we were guided by Mrs Stapleton to the point where they had found a pathway through the bog.

Only once we saw a trace that someone had passed that **perilous** way before us.

Holmes sank as he stepped from the path.

Sir Henry's missing boot.

Somewhere in the heart of the great Grimpen Mire, down in the foul slime which had sucked him in, this cold and cruel-hearted man is for ever buried.

perilous – dangerous

Holmes and Watson return to London. In his home at 221b Baker Street, Holmes goes over the case of the Hound of the Baskervilles.

This fellow, was a son of Rodger Baskerville, the younger brother of Sir Charles, who fled to South America. Stapleton married Beryl Garcia, changed his name to Vandeleur, established a school in Yorkshire.

The school **sank into infamy**. The Vandeleurs found it convenient to change their name to Stapleton.

The fellow found that only two lives intervened between him and a valuable estate. His ingenious mind suggested a way by which the baronet could be done to death. The dog he bought in London from dealers. It was the strongest and most savage **in their possession**.

He put pressure on Mrs Lyons to write this letter, **imploring** the old man for an interview on the evening before his departure for London. He then prevented her from going.

Driving back from Coombe Tracey, he was in time to get his hound. The dog sprang over the gate and pursued the unfortunate baronet. He fell dead at the end of the alley from heart disease and terror.

This fellow – Stapleton **sank into infamy** – got a bad reputation
in their possession – they owned **imploring** – begging

It is possible that Stapleton did not know of Henry Baskerville. Stapleton's first idea was that this young stranger might be done to death in London. He distrusted his wife. It was for this reason he took her to London. He kept his wife imprisoned in her room while he, disguised in a beard, followed Dr Mortimer. His wife dare not write to warn the man whom she knew to be in danger. She **adopted the expedient of cutting** out the words which would form the message.

It was essential for Stapleton to get some article of Sir Henry's so that, in case he was driven to use the dog, he might always have the means of setting him upon his track. By chance, the first boot was a new one and therefore useless.

What became of the hound when its master was in London?

There was an old manservant at Merripit House. This man has escaped from the country. It was he who cared for the hound, though he may never have known the purpose for which the beast was used. The hound was being kept in the outhouse on the evening that Sir Henry was coming to dinner.

adopted the expedient of cutting – decided to cut

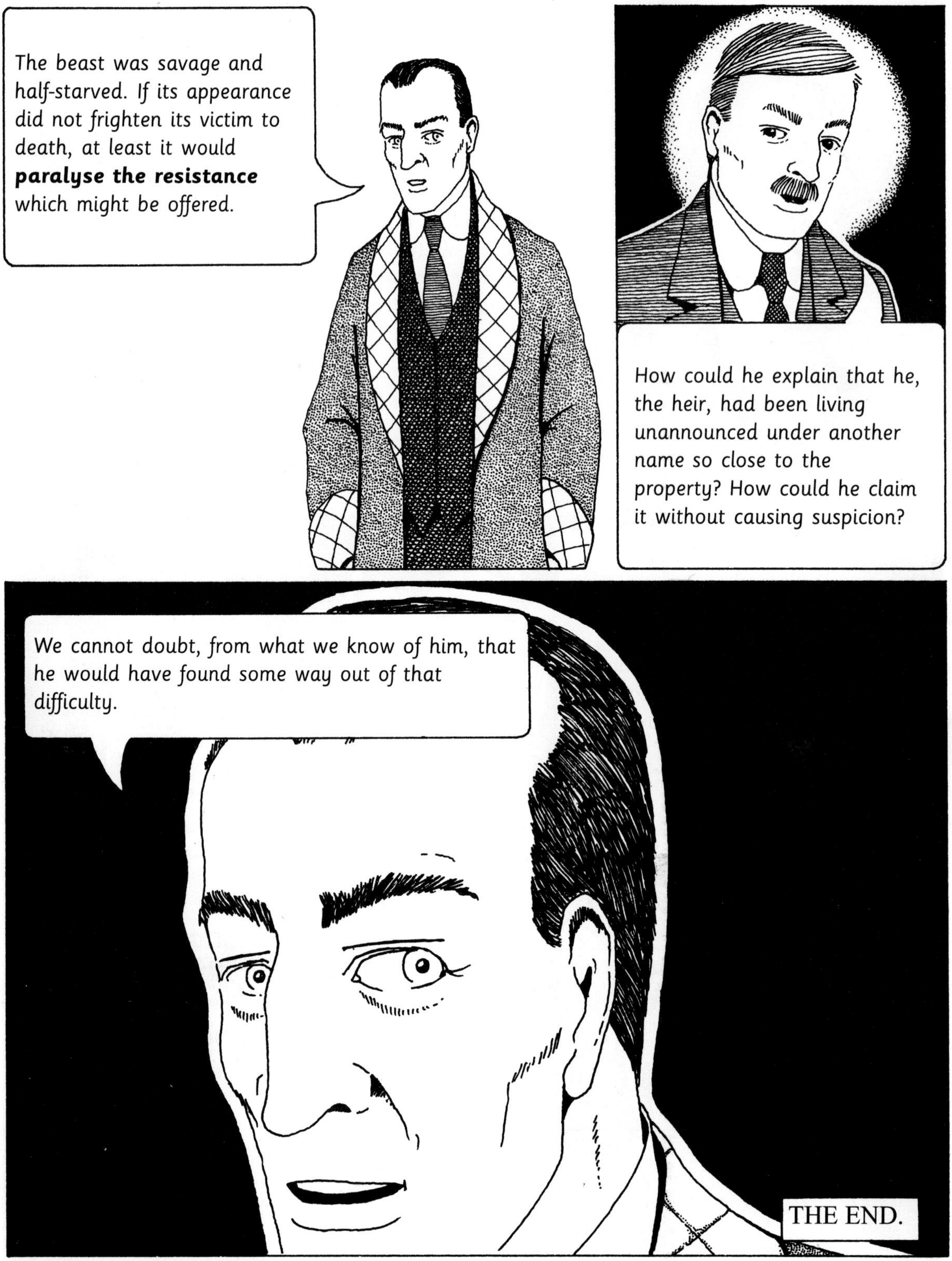

paralyse the resistance – stop him putting up a fight